THE LITTLE ROCK NINE
CHALLENGE SEGREGATION

COURAGEOUS KIDS OF THE CIVIL RIGHTS MOVEMENT

by Myra Faye Turner

illustrated by Dolo Okecki

CAPSTONE PRESS
a capstone imprint

Published by Capstone Press, an imprint of Capstone.
1710 Roe Crest Drive North Mankato, Minnesota 56003
capstonepub.com

Library of Congress Cataloging-in-Publication Data is available on the Library of Congress website.
Names: Turner, Myra Faye, author. | Okecki, Dolo, illustrator.
Title: The Little Rock nine challenge segregation : courageous kids of the civil rights movement / by Myra Faye Turner ; illustrated by Dolo Okecki.
Description: North Mankato, Minnesota : Capstone Press, 2023. | Series: Courageous kids | Includes bibliographical references and index. | Audience: Ages 8–11 | Audience: Grades 4–6
Summary: "In 1954, the U.S. Supreme Court ruled that schools had to allow Black students to attend previously all-white schools. On September 4, 1957, nine Black students were set to attend Little Rock Central High in Little Rock, Arkansas. But when they arrived, an angry mob of white people spat at them and hurled racist insults. They were also prevented from entering the school by the National Guard. After they were finally allowed in weeks later, they faced even more abuse from white students and staff. Discover the courage displayed by the Little Rock Nine as they fought to get an education while enduring terrible racism"—Provided by publisher.
Identifiers: LCCN 2021058799 (print) | LCCN 2021058800 (ebook) | ISBN 9781666334425 (hardcover) | ISBN 9781666334449 (paperback) | ISBN 9781666334432 (pdf) | ISBN 9781666334463 (kindle edition)
Subjects: LCSH: School integration—Arkansas—Little Rock—History—20th century—Juvenile literature. | Central High School (Little Rock, Ark.)—History—20th century—Juvenile literature. | African American high school students—Arkansas—Little Rock—History—20th century—Juvenile literature.
Classification: LCC LC214.23.L56 T87 2023 (print) | LCC LC214.23.L56 (ebook) | DDC 379.2/630976773—dc23
LC record available at https://lccn.loc.gov/2021058799
LC ebook record available at https://lccn.loc.gov/2021058800

All internet sites appearing in back matter were available and accurate when this book was sent to press.

EDITOR
Aaron Sautter

DESIGNER
Brann Garvey

MEDIA RESEARCHER
Morgan Walters

PRODUCTION SPECIALIST
Polly Fisher

Direct quotations appear in **bold italicized text** on the following pages:

Pages 11, 14, 18, 19, 22, 23, 26: from *The Long Shadow of Little Rock: A Memoir* by Daisy Bates. Fayetteville, AR: University of Arkansas Press, 1987.

Page 20: from *Warriors Don't Cry* by Melba Patillo Beals. Old Saybrook, CN: Tantor Media, 2014.

Page 29: from "The Youngest of the Little Rock Nine Speaks About Holding on to History," by Allison Keyes, *Smithsonian Magazine*, September 5, 2017, https://www.smithsonianmag.com/smithsonian-institution/youngest-little-rock-nine-speaks-about-holding-onto-history-180964732/

TABLE OF CONTENTS

THE JIM CROW SOUTH

The end of the U.S. Civil War (1861–1865) brought changes to the nation. Some changes were good. Enslaved Black people were set free and became U.S. citizens. They could own land, earn a living for themselves, and vote in elections.

But not everyone was happy. Many white people in the South refused to treat Black people as their equals. Government officials didn't help. They wrote new laws to stop Black people from enjoying their newfound freedoms.

During the early 1900s, "Jim Crow" laws in the South stated what Black people could and could not do. Black people could use public places but had to stay separate from white people. They had to use different restrooms. They could drink only from separate water fountains. Black people even had to sit in the back of city buses.

Get yourself to the back, boy.

You know you don't belong up here.

The Jim Crow laws got their name from traveling shows where white actors painted their faces to make fun of Black people. Some skits featured a character called Jim Crow that was based on a real-life enslaved man. The Jim Crow laws enforced the idea of "separate but equal."

Jim Crow laws even kept Black and white students from going to the same schools.

Over time, people began to oppose the unfair laws. They asked the government to end Jim Crow. One important issue was school segregation.

Black and white kids should be able to go to the same schools.

It was a long, hard fight. Then in 1954, the U.S. Supreme Court ruled on an important case. In *Brown v. Board of Education of Topeka Kansas,* the court ordered public schools to desegregate. The judges ruled "separate but equal" was illegal.

STATE JOURNAL

SCHOOL SEGREGATION BANNED

Supreme Court Reto
Doctrine of Separat
but Equal Education

It was a major win for the Civil Rights Movement. But many schools and local governments in the South refused to obey. They went to court to try and keep Black and white students from learning together.

But their efforts failed. The courts ordered the schools to allow Black students to attend white schools.

However, white protesters wouldn't give up easily. In 1957, nine Black teens made history at Central High School in Little Rock, Arkansas. They bravely faced an angry crowd and many racist insults to become the first Black students at Central.

Keep Central white!

We don't want Black kids in our school.

THE LITTLE ROCK NINE

The Jim Crow South tried to keep Black and white students apart. Some brave people worked to bring them together. They went to the highest court for help.

NO MORE SEGREGATION IN SCHOOL

NO RACE MIXING

Our kids deserve a better education.

We won't go to school with Black kids.

Students at white schools had better books. Their classrooms had better supplies.

At Black schools, students often had to study from old books. They sat in broken chairs and wrote on broken desks.

Some Black schools didn't have playgrounds or lunchrooms. Even the buildings for Black schools were often worse than white schools.

After the *Brown v Board of Education* case, some schools obeyed the order. But others did not. One year after the ruling, the Little Rock school board crafted a plan. Integration would start in the fall of 1957.

But not all schools agreed with the plan. The board picked Central as a test school. Then young Black students in lower grades would be enrolled over the next six years.

Nine Black teens would attend Central High. They became known as the Little Rock Nine. They were chosen by Daisy Bates. She was president of the Arkansas chapter of the National Association for the Advancement of Colored People (NAACP).

The NAACP is a civil rights organization that works to protect the rights of African Americans.

Terrance Roberts

Gloria Ray

Jefferson Thomas

Melba Pattillo

Ernest Green

Carlotta Walls

Thelma Mothershed

Daisy Bates

Elizabeth Eckford

Minnijean Brown

Mrs. Bates was a newspaper publisher. She owned the *Arkansas State Press* with her husband Lucius Christopher (L.C.) Bates.

It was an important newspaper in the Black community.

Sixteen-year-old Ernest Green was the oldest of the Nine. He was the only senior. The teens were friends and grew up near each other. Jefferson Thomas lived half a block from Green.

You want to shoot some hoops later?

Not today. I have to practice my saxophone.

At fourteen, Carlotta Walls was the youngest of the teens.

If any of you want to go Central in the fall, sign this paper. Someone will call you later.

Here Carlotta. Are you signing up?

Of course. It's a good school.

Thelma Mothershed had a heart condition. Her parents were naturally worried about their daughter going to Central.

Are you sure you want to do this?

Yes. I'll be okay. I promise.

At first, about 80 Black students were interested in going to Central. By the next summer, the Little Rock School Board had picked 17 candidates. The head of the public schools met with the students and their parents. He explained what to expect.

You won't be able to go to any football or basketball games or play any sports . . .

We can't do anything but go to class?

We may as well stay where we are.

Some of the students chose to stay at their own school. But nine of them wanted to go to a better school.

The date was set: September 4, 1957. Central High School would begin admitting Black students.

Mrs. Bates picked the teens because she felt they could handle the tough crowd. Still, the brave kids needed to prepare for the worst. So she taught them how to react in unfriendly settings.

Hey boy, go back to your own school where you belong!

Remember, no matter how angry you get, do not answer. Keep calm, look straight ahead, and walk away.

No one knew what to expect. But segregationist groups would likely cause trouble. They fought to keep the races apart.

We mothers are afraid to send our kids to Central. We heard both the white and Black kids are forming gangs. They have knives and guns. Someone's going to get hurt.

In August, the Mothers League of Little Rock Central High School went to court. They asked a judge to keep Black students out of Central. The group won their lawsuit. But it was overturned the next day in a Federal Court.

Labor Day signaled the last day of summer vacation for students. At the Bates's house, the day had been pleasant and quiet. Jefferson Thomas had even stopped by for a visit. But around 7:00 p.m. that evening, Mrs. Bates got some unexpected news.

Mrs. Bates, do you know that national guardsmen are surrounding Central High?

Mrs. Bates and her husband raced to the school.

National guardsmen are surrounding Central High School. No one is certain what this means. Governor Faubus will speak later this evening.

The day before the students were to enter Central, the head of schools called a meeting. He told the parents that it would be easier to protect the students without the adults there.

Mrs. Bates instead arranged for some pastors to meet the students a few blocks from the school. They'd walk with the students to help keep them safe.

Mrs. Bates asked if she could join the students, but she didn't get an answer until much later. It was after midnight when she finally called the students.

However, Elizabeth Eckford's family didn't have a telephone. Mrs. Bates would have to find another way to reach Elizabeth the next day.

We'll meet at Twelfth and Park at 8:30 a.m.

The next morning, Melba Pattillo couldn't get to the meeting spot. The street was thick with traffic and protesters. Melba and her mother decided to park and walk the last several blocks to meet the others.

Just keep looking forward, baby.

As Melba and her mother walked through the crowd, they heard racial insults cutting through the air. Melba strained to see what the fuss was about and saw her friend.

Get out of here!

We don't want your kind!

Elizabeth!

Elizabeth was the first student to arrive at the school. Mrs. Bates had forgotten to contact the teen. She had to face the angry mob alone.

Go home!

Go back to where you belong!

Arkansas Governor Orval Faubus had called in the National Guard. He claimed the soldiers were there to protect the Black teens. But it was a lie. He had actually called them in to stop the students from entering the school.

You can't go into the school.

Eckford tried to break through the line of soldiers. But they wouldn't budge. As the crowd closed in on her they shouted more racist insults. The soldiers did nothing to help the frightened teen.

Elizabeth turned around and walked to a bus stop. She wasn't sure where to go, but she knew she had to get away from the angry crowd. The mob followed her and surrounded the bench.

BUS STOP

I hope the bus comes soon.

Go on, girl! Get yourself back home!

Soon, two white people in the crowd stepped in. One was Dr. Benjamin Fine, a reporter with the *New York Times*.

Don't let them see you cry.

Another helper was Grace Lorch.

Y'all leave this child alone!

Dr. Fine and Ms. Lorch agreed that they had to get Elizabeth away from the angry mob. They walked across the street with her to use a pay phone to call a taxi.

As Dr. Fine waited on the sidewalk with Elizabeth, Lorch tried to enter the building. But the angry protesters wouldn't let her in to use the phone.

Let me pass.

Not as long as you're helping that girl.

Elizabeth's mother was a teacher at a school for blind and deaf children. Elizabeth decided to head there. Lorch took her to another nearby bus stop. When the bus arrived, Lorch got on with Elizabeth.

There, there. It's going to be okay. You're safe now.

As Elizabeth and Melba got away from the crowd, the other seven Black students arrived at Central High together. Four ministers walked with them. Mrs. Bates waited in the car. Meanwhile, a line of soldiers stood at attention as the street overflowed with angry white faces.

Go home!

Go back to Africa!

I'm sorry, but I can't let you enter.

Why?

Governor Faubus has ordered it.

Once again, the group had to face the angry crowd as they returned to the car.

Y'all don't belong here!

Keep Central High white!

Orval Faubus and his wife once published a newspaper called the *Madison County Record*. He sometimes wrote articles about education. Before entering politics, Faubus had been a teacher.

Faubus first ran for governor in 1954. Many said he couldn't win. He was unknown and didn't have much political experience.

VOTE FOR FAUBUS
RIEND OF THE
NORKI MAN

. . . Arkansas is not ready for a complete and sudden mixing of the races in public schools . . .

But when segregationists opposed the *Brown v Board of Education* ruling, the governor took notice. The one-time teacher decided to stand with them to get their support—and their votes.

When Faubus won the election, his victory surprised a lot of people. He became very popular in the state. Faubus eventually served six terms as governor.

Labor Day Press Conference, September 2, 1957

I have been told white supremacists are on their way to Little Rock. I've called in the troops to protect Central High.

But instead of keeping the peace, the governor's words on Labor Day caused more harm. A lot of white people were already angry. His words made them angrier.

He said there would be trouble if the Black students tried to enter Central High School.

. . . blood will run in the streets of Little Rock.

On September 4, the governor stopped the students from entering Central. But it wasn't good enough for some white people. That night, angry crowds roamed the city, protesting and bullying Black residents.

Keep your kids out of our schools—or there'll be real trouble!

People called up the students on the phone to harass and threaten them.

Hello.

Melba?

Yes.

I know where you live. We gonna get you tonight . . . 'long about midnight.

That night, the students waited to learn their next move.

We think it would be better to not send you back to Central right now. Our lawyers are going to court. We're asking the judge to remove the soldiers.

For the next three weeks, NAACP lawyers, including Thurgood Marshall, fought for the students in court. Marshall later became the first Black judge on the U.S. Supreme Court.

Your honor, Black students should have the same quality education as white students. We ask you to order the governor to remove the troops and let the students in to Central.

In the meantime, President Dwight D. Eisenhower got involved.

I ask you again, please remove the soldiers. Let the Black students enter.

I'm sorry sir. I cannot do that. The guards are there to protect the students.

Finally, on September 20, Federal judge Ronald Davies ordered the soldiers to be removed from the school. Governor Faubus realized that his fight was over.

I will obey the judge's order. The soldiers will be removed. Tomorrow, the Little Rock police will take over and provide security.

BRAVE WARRIORS

On September 23, 1957, as the students prepared to go to Central High, the threat of violence hung in the air.

We won't stand for our schools being integrated.

The teens were escorted to the school by the Little Rock police. To avoid the crowd, they entered through a side door.

They're in!

The angry crowd tried to push their way into the school. Fearing for the students' safety, the police slipped them out through a delivery entrance at the back of the school.

Keep your heads down until I tell you it's clear.

Mrs. Bates was later asked what would happen next.

Will the kids return to school?

They are going to remain out of school until the President of the United States guarantees their protection within Central High.

That night, things grew even more dangerous. White mobs roamed the streets. Adults dragged Black people from their cars and beat them. Teenagers threw bottles and bricks at houses in Black neighborhoods

Little Rock's mayor, Woodrow Mann, needed help. He called the president.

Mr. President, the situation is getting out of control. I'm afraid one of the children will get hurt.

The president sent help. A force of 1,200 paratroopers called the "Screaming Eagles" took over from the police.

On September 25, 1957, the Little Rock Nine arrived at Central High School for the third time. Reporters filled the streets. A crowd had gathered, but they didn't cause trouble.

At 9:22 a.m. the students made history. The Little Rock Nine, along with 22 soldiers, walked into Central High School.

Inside, some students were friendly toward the Black students. Some white students showed little interest. They didn't bully the students, but they also didn't welcome them.

I heard you're a good singer. Would you like to join our glee club?

Yes, I'd love to.

Some of the white teachers were hostile to the Nine. They refused to teach them. But others were helpful.

I'll help you catch up on the work you missed.

Thank you, ma'am.

But not everyone was nice at the school. Some students bullied the Black students. One white girl dropped trash in Carlotta Walls's lunch. Another student hit Jefferson Thomas and knocked him out.

Why don't you take yourself out of our school with the rest of the trash?

In early October the paratroopers were removed from inside the school. The Arkansas National Guard took over. Unlike the paratroopers, some guardsmen looked the other way when the Black students were bullied.

Ha! You dropped your books, boy.

One day a gang of white students took over the school and attacked the Nine. It took a few hours to get things under control. Mrs. Bates called the army general in charge.

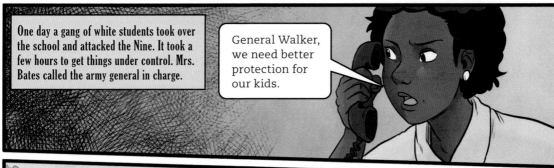

General Walker, we need better protection for our kids.

The general assigned two troopers to each of the Nine. The soldiers walked the students to class each day. They couldn't punish the bullies.

But the soldiers couldn't be with the Nine in their classrooms or at lunch. This allowed the bullying to continue. Still, the soldiers' presence made things better for the Black students.

The Nine had handled the hostility at the school well. However, one day in January 1958, Minnijean became fed up with the bullying. So she fought back. The school suspended her for six days.

I'm tired of y'all bullying me!

After her suspension, Minnijean agreed to not fight back, even when being bullied. But the next month a student threw her purse at Minnijean. She threw it back. The school then suspended her for the rest of the year.

Why don't you leave me alone?

But there was also good news. Ernest Green made history again. In May 1958, he became the first Black student to graduate from Central High School.

Ernest G. Green.

However, trouble was still brewing.

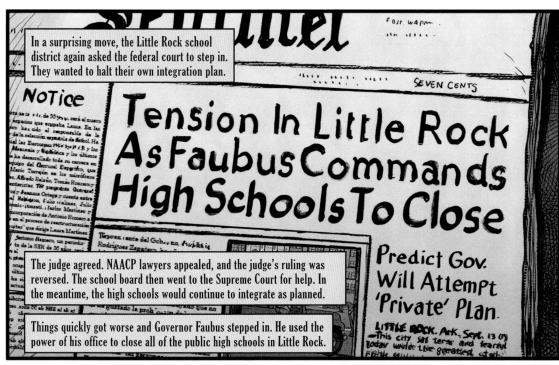

In a surprising move, the Little Rock school district again asked the federal court to step in. They wanted to halt their own integration plan.

Tension In Little Rock As Faubus Commands High Schools To Close

Predict Gov. Will Attempt 'Private' Plan.

LITTLE ROCK, Ark, Sept. 13 09 —This city sat tense and fearful today while the greatest...

The judge agreed. NAACP lawyers appealed, and the judge's ruling was reversed. The school board then went to the Supreme Court for help. In the meantime, the high schools would continue to integrate as planned.

Things quickly got worse and Governor Faubus stepped in. He used the power of his office to close all of the public high schools in Little Rock.

The high schools remained closed for a year while the adults battled over integration. When the U.S. Supreme court finally ruled on the case, the segregationists lost.

The schools were reopened in 1959. Today Central High and schools across the United States are fully integrated—thanks to the courage of nine brave students who made it possible.

The Little Rock Nine are important civil rights icons. They paved the way for Black students to get a better education. Because of their bravery, more schools throughout the South were integrated.

Their actions inspired others, young and old, to fight against injustice. Decades later, they still inspire new generations.

The Nine later got jobs in many different fields. In the 1970s, Ernest Green worked for President Jimmy Carter. Minnijean Brown later worked for President Bill Clinton.

Melba Pattillo became a reporter. Thelma Mothershed went on to become a school teacher and counselor. Elizabeth Eckford and Jefferson Thomas both served in the army. Carlotta Walls ran a real estate business.

Gloria Ray was the founder and editor of a successful computer magazine. Terrence Roberts became a psychologist. As of 2021, eight of the nine students were still alive. Jefferson Thomas died of cancer in 2010.

In 1999, President Bill Clinton awarded each of the Little Rock Nine the Congressional Gold Medal. The medal is the highest award a civilian can receive. It's given for outstanding service to the country.

When recalling the events at Central High School, the Nine admit how hard it was for them. However, they're proud of their role in advancing the Civil Rights Movement.

Carlotta Walls, who was the youngest, expressed it best:

It was not an easy task, but we didn't expect it to be as it turned out. You have to learn how to deal with adversity, and I think we all did.

GLOSSARY

civil rights (SI-vil RYTS)—the rights that all people have to freedom and equal treatment under the law

desegregate (dee-SEG-ruh-gayt)—to end the practice of keeping people apart based on their race

integrate (IN-tuh-grate)—to bring people of different races together in schools and other public places

paratrooper (PAIR-uh-troop-uhr)—a soldier trained to jump by parachute into battle

psychologist (sye-KAHL-uh-jist)—a doctor who studies people's minds and emotions and treats patients with mental or emotional troubles

quality (KWAHL-uh-tee)—very good or having high value

segregation (seg-ruh-GAY-shuhn)—the practice of keeping groups of people apart, especially based on their race

skit (SKIT)—a short play that is often funny

white supremacist (WITE soo-PREM-uh-sist)—someone who believes the white race is better than all other races

READ MORE

Loureiro, Stephanie. *Fighting for Civil Rights*. Huntington Beach, CA: Teacher Created Material, 2019.

Smith, Sherri I. *What Is the Civil Rights Movement?*. New York: Penguin Random House, 2020.

Turner, Myra Faye. *Ruby Bridges Takes Her Seat: Courageous Kid of the Civil Rights Movement*. North Mankato, Minnesota: Capstone, 2023.

INTERNET SITES

Britannica Kids: Brown v. Board of Education of Topeka
kids.britannica.com/kids/article/Brown-v-Board-of-Education-of-Topeka/627788

History for Kids: Little Rock Nine Crisis Facts for Kids
historyforkids.org/little-rock-nine-crisis/

The Little Rock Nine
upfront.scholastic.com/issues/2017-18/090417/the-little-rock-nine.html#1210L

Time for Kids: Justice for All
timeforkids.com/g34/little-rock-nine/

INDEX

ABOUT THE AUTHOR

Myra Faye Turner is a poet and author living in New Orleans, Louisiana. She has written for adults but prefers writing for young readers. She has written over two dozen nonfiction books for children and young adults. Topics covered include politics, the Apollo moon landing, edible insects, nature, STEM, firefighting robots, and U.S. and African-American history.